Questions *from the* Answer

Conversations with Jesus that Shape the Soul

by
Jon Lands

— • ◆ • —

"He that hath ears to hear, let him hear."
—MATTHEW 11:15

Gethsemane
PRESS

Gethsemane
P R E S S

Questions from the Answer: Conversations with Jesus that Shape the Soul
by Jonathan E. Lands

Copyright © 2025 by Jonathan E. Lands
All Rights Reserved.

Published in Nashville, Tennessee, by Gethsemane Press.

Hardcover ISBN: 979-8-9992446-0-4
eBook ISBN: 979-8-9992446-2-8

*For more resources by Jon Lands
go to www.AGoodWord.net*

Printed in the United States of America

TABLE OF CONTENTS

PREFACE

Jesus is not just an answer—He is *the* Answer.

The Answer to our sin, our sorrow, our suffering. The Answer to our longings, our questions, our fears. He is the Savior who rescues us, the Shepherd who leads us, and the King who reigns over every storm. He is our Peace when we are anxious, our Light when we are lost, and our Strength when we are weak. In a world filled with uncertainty, there is one unwavering truth: *Jesus is the Answer to every need and every concern of life.*

I didn't come to this study with a plan to write—I came as a soul trying to listen. It began in a season when my own questions outnumbered my clarity. Questions about direction. About timing. About trust. And as I sat with Scripture, something caught my eye: Jesus asked questions, too. A lot of them. Not because He needed information—He is, after all, the Omniscient One—but because He longed to give revelation. His questions weren't flung into the air to fill silence; they were crafted to stir the soul. They reached into corners of my heart I hadn't fully opened. And what began as quiet curiosity became a deeper invitation. This book is the fruit of that journey.

Here's the wonder that still amazes me: the One who *is* the Answer didn't simply walk through life handing out conclusions. He asked questions. The Gospels record Jesus asking more than 300 questions during His earthly ministry.

People asked Him 183 questions, but He gave direct answers to only three. Three!

Why would the One who is the Answer lead with questions?

Because Jesus knew that questions stir what answers often settle. His questions weren't for His benefit—they were for ours. They reached past the surface and touched the soul. They weren't meant to inform the mind alone but to transform the heart.

"Why are you so afraid?"
"Why do you worry?"
"Do you love Me?"

Each question was—and still is—an invitation to reflect, wrestle, and draw nearer to the Answer Himself.

Rooted in the Jewish tradition of learning through inquiry, Jesus used questions not merely as a teaching tool but as a transformational encounter. Like rays of light piercing through clouds, His questions broke through confusion, exposed hidden fears, and opened the way to deeper faith.

These questions are not just historical echoes from the hills of Galilee or the courts of Jerusalem. They are alive. They still speak. And they still invite. So come—listen closely. Let His questions linger.

Let them search you, soften you, strengthen you. Because questions from *the Answer* will not leave you unchanged. They are His way of drawing you into something deeper.

Deeper trust. Deeper love. Deeper surrender.

Are you ready to respond?

CHAPTER ONE

The Question of Desire and Spiritual Hunger

"Then Jesus turned, and saw them following, a
nd saith unto them, What seek ye?"
—JOHN 1:38

———————— • ◆ • ————————

It began on a dusty path near the Jordan River. The wilderness still hummed with the echoes of John the Baptist's preaching, and two former fishermen had just left behind the only teacher they'd ever known. The air held both tension and anticipation—the kind that lingers when one voice fades and your heart strains to hear another.

They didn't hesitate. With hearts stirred by something deeper than spectacle, they took their first steps after Him.

A Question That Stops You in Your Tracks

It was not a sermon that drew them. Not a miracle. Not even a call. Just a sentence—six quiet words spoken by a wilderness prophet with sun-leathered skin and wild conviction: "Behold the Lamb of God." That was all. No fanfare. No altar call. No signs in the sky or flashes of thunder. Just a pointing finger and a sacred name. And that, somehow, was enough.

John the Baptist didn't hold them back. He didn't clutch their sleeves or ask them to stay one day more. He didn't demand loyalty or permission slips. He simply did what every faithful preacher hopes to do—he pointed to Someone greater and stepped aside. That's the sacred task of every voice in the wilderness: to direct attention, not gather it.

And so, the two men followed.

They didn't say a word. They simply started walking behind Jesus. No introductions. No credentials. No clarifying questions. Just footsteps echoing on a dusty road. Two shadows following the Light of the world.

Then it happened. Jesus stopped. Turned. Faced them. His eyes met theirs—not with suspicion or surprise, but with the calm intensity of a soul who sees straight through skin and sinew to what a man carries deep within.

And then He spoke.

He asked a question—not just any question, but the first one ever recorded from His lips in the Gospel of John. It wasn't rhetorical. It wasn't evasive. It was piercing.

"What seek ye?"

Let that settle in. His first words to His first followers weren't a command, a parable, or a promise. They were a question.

He didn't ask, "Who are you?"
He didn't ask, "Do you believe in Me?"
He didn't even ask, "Are you ready to leave everything behind?"
He simply asked, "What are you looking for?"

Of all the things the Son of God could have said at that moment, He chose a question that goes to the very heart of human longing. Because that's what Jesus does. He doesn't start with doctrine. He begins with desire. With the ache under the armor. He listens for the longing beneath our ambition, the stirring that success can't silence. Jesus doesn't speak to our roles or reputations—He speaks to the desires we dare not name.

It is a question that reaches across centuries and cultures. A question that doesn't age. A question not just for them, but for you and me. It has found its way into sanctuaries and subway cars, into hospital waiting rooms and lonely bedrooms. It is the question that whispers to every soul brave enough to follow Him:

What seek ye?

We live in a world full of seekers. Everyone is chasing something. Some chase significance. Others chase comfort. Some pursue security. Others pursue sensation. And most of us, if we're honest, are chasing some blurry combination of all the above—hoping the right job, or the right partner, or the right number in our bank account will finally still the trembling in our souls.

The tragedy, of course, is not that we fail to find what we're chasing. The tragedy is that we often chase the wrong thing to begin with.

What do you seek?

Do you seek a position? He offers you a cross.
Do you seek a platform? He gives a basin and towel.
Do you seek a miracle? He offers a message.
Do you seek a roadmap? He offers Himself.

Jesus never came to baptize our ambitions. He came to transform them. And so, His first question isn't about readiness or righteousness or resolve—it's about the real hunger beneath it all. When He asks, "What seek ye?" He's not offering a better version of your dream. He's inviting you to lay it down. To trade what you think will satisfy for what truly will. Because the deepest hunger of your heart won't be filled by success or applause or even a good plan—it will only be filled by Him.

An Invitation That Changes Everything

The two men—one of whom was Andrew, the brother of Peter, and the other likely John himself—stood there, probably caught off guard. What do you say to the One you're unsure how to approach? They didn't have a rehearsed answer. So they did what honest seekers do: they asked a question in return.

"Rabbi, where dwellest thou?"

At first glance, it sounds like small talk. But it isn't. Their question wasn't about location. It was about relationships. What they were really asking was, "Can we be with You? Can we walk beside You, listen to You, learn from You? We don't just want to know about You—we want to know You."

They weren't looking for an explanation. They were hoping for an invitation.

And that's exactly what they received.

Jesus replied with three simple words: "Come and see."

He didn't give directions. He didn't outline next steps or hand them a doctrinal statement. He simply invited them to be with Him. Come and see. Come not only with your feet but with your heart. Come with your doubts. Come with your questions. Come, not because you have everything figured out—but because you don't.

So they came. They followed Him down that dusty path to the place where He was staying, and John tells us they remained with Him that day.

It was about the tenth hour, he says.

That detail might seem unimportant. But it's the kind of note you include when something unforgettable happens. John didn't forget the hour because it was the hour everything changed. It was the hour when following became abiding. When curiosity turned into communion. When they stopped chasing answers and started walking with the Answer Himself.

Imagine the moment. The sun dipping low on the horizon, painting the sky with strokes of fire and gold. The shadows stretching long. A small, makeshift home—humble, unassuming. The Son of God, seated perhaps beside a flickering flame, speaking softly. Not preaching. Not performing. Just being. Listening to their wonder. Asking what mattered most. Revealing Himself not through spectacle, but through presence.

They stayed until the sky turned violet, and the stars crept in like quiet witnesses. They stayed until the world fell still, and the only sound was the crackle of the fire and the whisper of their hearts saying, "This is what we've been waiting for."

They came seeking something.
They found Someone.
And that changed everything.

A Moment That Marks a Life

We know how the story unfolds from there. Andrew, overflowing with excitement, ran to find his brother Simon. "We have found the Messiah," he said. And that simple statement, born out of a day spent in the presence of Jesus, would set into motion a chain of events that would change the world.

Because one man heard.
One man followed.
One man stayed.

And out of that quiet moment came the man we would one day know as Peter—the rock. The preacher of Pentecost. The author of epistles. The fisherman turned fisher of men.

You never know what God will build out of one moment of seeking.

Which brings us back to the question.

Jesus still stops. He still turns. He still looks. And with those same tender eyes, He still asks each of us: What seek ye?

What are you hoping will finally fill the ache?
What are you pursuing that you believe will make you whole?

Do you seek peace? He is your peace.
Do you seek purpose? He is your calling.
Do you seek truth? He is the way, the truth, and the life.

To the one who feels aimless—to the soul that has chased applause, affirmation, or acceptance and found it hollow—He is asking. Not with judgment. Not with disappointment. But with the gentle invitation of a Shepherd who knows how lost sheep feel.

What seek ye?

Not, "What have you done?"
Not, "What do you deserve?"
Just, "What are you after?"

You don't have to fix yourself to follow Him. You don't have to explain your motives or clean up your mess. He already knows. He's not looking for polish. He's looking for honesty. And maybe, just maybe, the answer you didn't even know you were giving is: "You. I'm seeking You."

John never forgot the hour. That moment marked him. When Jesus truly sees you—when He speaks to your longing—you don't forget the time of day, the scent of the air, the weight that lifted. You remember the way your heart stirred, the way time paused, the way everything changed without your knowing exactly how.

So here's the invitation:

Come and see.

Not once, but again. And again. And again.

Come and see Him in the pages of Scripture, where His voice still whispers through red letters and broken bread. Come and see Him in the quiet of prayer, in the tears of repentance, in the joy of grace rediscovered. Come and see Him in the places you thought too ordinary for glory.

Come and see that the One who asked, *"What seek ye?"* is also the One who *came to seek and to save that which was lost.*

And if you still don't know exactly what you're seeking—that's okay.

Start with Him.

Because when you seek Him, you will find Him.
And when you find Him, you will find everything else.

———————————— • ◆ • ————————————

The Answer Asks You...

- What are you truly seeking—beneath the goals, plans, and prayers?
- Have you ever mistaken the gifts of God for God Himself?
- What might Jesus be inviting you to leave behind to follow Him more fully?
- When was the last time you only abided with Jesus rather than pursued something from Him?
- Are you willing to follow Him without knowing exactly where He'll lead?

CHAPTER TWO

The Question of Identity and Personal Faith

"He saith unto them, But whom say ye that I am?"
—MATTHEW 16:15

———— • ◆ • ————

They were far from Jerusalem, far from the crowds and the noise of Galilee. In a place known for idols and ancient fear, Jesus chose a moment of quiet confrontation. The setting was provocative, the question piercing.

Where the Pagan Gods Once Stood

Caesarea Philippi was no neutral ground. It was a stronghold of shrines, a monument to confusion, a showcase of humanity's futile attempts to define the divine. There were niches in the rock wall for the idols of many gods, altars scattered like trophies from long-forgotten wars. And above it all loomed the cave known as the "Gate of Hades," where water gushed from the earth like breath from the underworld.

And there—right there—is where Jesus asked His disciples a question that turned dusty sandals into trembling feet.
"Whom do men say that I, the Son of Man, am?"

It was a disarming beginning. The question seemed simple, maybe even academic. What's the word on the street? What are people saying about Me? The disciples, probably relieved to speak factually, rattled off the latest buzz.

"Some say you're John the Baptist," one said. Another chimed in, "Others say Elijah." A third added, "Or maybe Jeremiah. Or one of the prophets."

A roll call of the greats—dead prophets repackaged for a hungry people who couldn't make sense of Jesus. They were grasping for categories, trying to pin the extraordinary into something they could explain. John. Elijah. Jeremiah. Close, but infinitely off the mark.

When the Question Turns Personal

And then the question turned.

"But whom say *ye* that I am?"

There are moments when the world fades, and only one voice matters. This was one of them. Jesus moved from the third person to the second. From "they" to "you." And suddenly, the question wasn't a poll—it was personal.

It always is.

Jesus never stops with the opinions of others. He turns to you, eye-level, heart-first. What about you? You've walked with Me. You've heard the wind obey My voice. You've seen water turn to wine and death reverse course. What do you say?

Simon Peter didn't flinch.

"Thou art the Christ, the Son of the living God."

There it was. Like sunrise after a sleepless night. Like clarity cutting through fog. A fisherman just answered the riddle of eternity.

A Confession Revealed from Heaven

And oh, what a proclamation it was.

"Thou art the Christ"—not a teacher, not a prophet, not a second coming of someone else. The Christ. The Anointed One. The long-awaited Messiah, not wrapped in royalty but veiled in humanity.

"The Son of the living God"—not fashioned by human hands, not entombed in a cave, not a myth draped in legend. Living. Active. Present. God, not in the abstract, but alive—and this Man, His Son.

Peter's voice must have echoed against the pagan stones, rattling the silence like thunder against the cliffs. And Jesus, I imagine, smiled—not because Peter figured it out, but because heaven had opened and truth had landed.

Peter's response came quickly—too quickly, perhaps, for him to fully grasp the weight of what he had just said.

There was no hesitation in him, no stumbling over the words, no furrowed brow of theological analysis. The words leaped from his lips as if they had been waiting in the wings of his heart, rehearsed by heaven and loosed by grace.

When Grace Puts Words in Our Mouth

And that's just like Peter, isn't it?

He speaks before he thinks. He jumps before he looks. He blurts out what others only whisper. Sometimes, that makes a mess of things—but not this time. This time, it made history.

Because in this moment, Peter didn't just say something true. He said something revealed. His lips moved, but it was God who had formed the words. The confession came through him but not from him.

Jesus confirmed it:
"Blessed art thou... for flesh and blood hath not revealed it unto thee, but my Father which is in heaven."

That matters. Because faith is not merely intellectual assent or logical deduction. It is not a conclusion we arrive at on our own. It is divine illumination. It is grace reaching into dust and breathing revelation. It is a Father whispering to His child.

And if we're honest—really honest—most of us are more like Peter than we'd care to admit.

We know what it is to get it wrong. We've made promises we couldn't keep. We've stepped out of boats and sunk beneath fear. We've drawn swords in misguided zeal and wept bitterly in regret. And yet—despite all that—we've had moments. Moments when heaven broke through our fumbling and frailty, and we saw Jesus clearly. Moments when the words came, not because we had studied well but because the Father had spoken softly.

Peter was not always consistent, but in this moment, he was right. And sometimes, being right about Jesus—seeing Him for who He is—is enough to change everything.

Seeing Him... and Finding Ourselves

And then, Jesus said something that must have stunned Peter more than his own confession:

"Thou art Peter, and upon this rock I will build my church."

It was as if Jesus were saying, "You see Me clearly—and now let Me show you who you are." That's the power of His question: it doesn't just search your heart—it reveals His. And suddenly, as you discover Him—you begin to discover yourself. Not the version of you shaped by failures or fears, but the one shaped by your faith in Him.

But this scene isn't the end—it's the beginning of something even more glorious.

Just days later, Jesus will take Peter, James, and John up a mountain. Not just any mountain, but the Mount of Transfiguration. And there—only after this confession—He will peel back the veil. He will shine in glory. His face will dazzle like the sun, and His clothes will radiate with light. Moses and Elijah will appear. Heaven will speak again.

Before the brilliance of the mountaintop, there was the quiet weight of a question. Glory doesn't precede identity. It follows it.

Because you cannot see Jesus in His glory until you've answered the question: *Who do you say that I am?*

He Still Asks

It's not a riddle to solve. It's not a theory to discuss. It is the door through which we all must walk.

And here's the truth—Jesus doesn't ask it because He needs to know.

He asks it because *you* do. So let's return to that moment—not as spectators, but as participants.

Jesus turns, eyes searching—not the crowd, not the culture—but you.

"But whom say ye that I am?"

He's not asking for a borrowed answer or a rehearsed reply. He's asking for your heart.

Not what your church says. Not what your parents believe. Not what the world assumes. But what you say. Because until you say it—until *you* say it—you'll stand just outside the brilliance of His glory.

But the moment you do… The moment your heart rises and your voice responds with the trembling certainty of Peter— "You are the Christ." That's when everything changes. That's when the veil lifts. That's when the mountaintop comes into view.

That's when you begin to see—not just the man from Nazareth, not just the healer or teacher—but the Lord of Glory, standing where gods once stood, shining with the light that no darkness can overcome.

He still asks.

In the quiet places of your heart, far from the voices of others— He asks again, not with pressure, but with love:

"But whom say ye that I am?"

—————————— • ◆ • ——————————

The Answer Asks You...

- What voices have shaped your understanding of who Jesus is—culture, family, tradition? Have you ever stopped to make your own confession?
- Why do you think Jesus asked this question in a place filled with false gods instead of the temple in Jerusalem?
- Have you experienced a moment when God revealed something about Christ to you—not from logic, but from the heart?
- What would change if you lived every day with the certainty that Jesus is the Christ, the Son of the living God?
- Who do **you** say He is—and what does your answer reveal about who you are becoming?

CHAPTER THREE

The Question of Gratitude and Forgotten Grace

"And Jesus answering said, Were there not ten
cleansed? But where are the nine?"
—LUKE 17:17

• ◆ •

It happened on the road.

Not in the temple. Not in the synagogue. Not in the quiet of
a Galilean hillside. But somewhere between Galilee and
Samaria—a place that sat awkwardly on the map and even
more awkwardly in the hearts of most Jews. It was a stretch of
land where identities blurred, prejudices simmered, and
travelers, if they could help it, kept moving.

Jesus was moving, too—headed toward Jerusalem, toward
destiny. But in this moment, His steps slowed. Not because of
geography but because of humanity. Because just outside a
village, a voice cried out.

Make that ten voices.

Desperate Voices on the Borderline

"Jesus, Master, have mercy on us!"

They did not approach Him; they couldn't. Their condition made it illegal and unthinkable. They were lepers—outcasts in a world that mistook illness for sin and broken skin for a broken soul. They were required to keep their distance, to ring a bell, or shout a warning whenever someone came too close.

But this time, they did the shouting for another reason: not to warn Jesus away, but to call Him near.

There's a kind of desperation that has no time for eloquence. No time for proof of worth. These ten men had been stripped of everything—families, jobs, names, futures. All they had left was their voices, and they used them. Ten voices joined in a single, trembling request: "Have mercy."

What's fascinating is what they didn't say.

They didn't ask to be healed. Didn't lay out a plan or point out symptoms. They left the shape of mercy up to the One they called "Master."

It was enough.

Jesus didn't touch them. He didn't say, "Be cleansed," as in other healings. He gave an instruction: "Go show yourselves unto the priests."

Strange, isn't it?

The law required healed lepers to show themselves to the priest as proof of cleansing. But these men weren't healed yet. Their skin still bore the rot. Their limbs still carried the stench of death. And yet Jesus said, "Go."

And they went.

Obedience on Unhealed Feet

One foot in front of the other. Perhaps hesitant at first. Possibly wondering if this, too, would end in disappointment. But somewhere along that road—maybe after the first mile, maybe the fifth—one of them noticed. His hand, once mangled and oozing, was whole. Another saw that his foot, once twisted and numb, could now bear weight. Another felt warmth return to his face. And then, one by one, they saw it.

They were healed.

Ten were healed.

But only one came back.

The Unexpected Worshipper

He turned around. Left the path to the priest. Ran—not walked—back to the feet of Jesus.

And he fell down. Loudly. Joyfully. Gratefully.

A man once banished, now bowing before the One who gave him back his life.

He didn't care about protocol. Didn't wait to be invited. Didn't worry who was watching. He had been living on the outskirts of existence, a man with no place to go and no one to welcome him when he arrived. But now? He came rushing back—not to a synagogue, not to a priest, not to a family reunion—but to Jesus.

He collapsed at His feet with tears in his throat and worship in his breath.

And Luke, the physician with a theologian's pen, adds a detail that punches through the page like a thunderclap: "And he was a Samaritan."

Not a Jew. Not a son of the covenant. Not one who had grown up reciting psalms in the synagogue or waiting for the Messiah. He was an outsider among outsiders. A leper, yes—but a Samaritan leper. If leprosy had made him unclean, his nationality had made him unwelcome. To the Jewish world, he was a stranger in every sense—a man unfit to stand in the temple or to sit at the table.

The Loudest Praise From the Lowest Place

He had the least reason to expect a miracle.

The least theological training to understand one.

The least cultural expectation to receive one.

And yet, he is the one whose heart erupted with thanks.

Isn't it striking that the man who had the least to lose in religious circles was the one who gave the most in praise? That the one furthest from the altar was the first to kneel? He knew, better than the others perhaps, that mercy is never earned, and grace is always astonishing.

The others may have felt entitled—children of Abraham, accustomed to blessings, perhaps believing that healing was a long-overdue justice.

But the Samaritan knew better.

He had no spiritual pedigree, no legal right to the Messiah, no passport into the promises of Israel. He was a man twice rejected—once by disease, once by bloodline.

And yet mercy had found him.

So he did the only thing a heart like his could do: he returned. He worshipped. He wept. He glorified God with a loud voice, not because he was louder by nature, but because grace had reached further to get to him.

He gave more because he knew he deserved nothing.

And Jesus, ever the master of the moment, looked around—not in confusion, but in grief. His voice didn't crack with surprise but with sorrow.

The Question That Still Echoes

"Were there not ten cleansed? But where are the nine?"
He asked, but He knew.

Nine received and ran. One received and returned.
And the one was a Samaritan.

It seems the further grace has to reach, the louder gratitude tends to be.

"Where are the nine?"—it's not just a question of numbers. It's a question of hearts.

Ten men received a miracle. Ten men were physically restored. But only one saw past the gift to the Giver. Only one turned a transaction into a relationship.

Healed, But Not Whole

They got what they wanted—and moved on.

How many of us do the same?

How often do we cry out in our pain and forget Him in our healing? How often do we treat God as a stepping stone rather than a Savior?

Gratitude, it seems, is rarer than miracles.

"Where are the nine?"—it's a rhetorical question, yes, but it's also an invitation. An invitation to self-examination. An invitation to recognize that healing isn't the end of the story. It's the beginning of worship.

And worship is what this Samaritan gave.

He didn't just say thank you. He glorified God with a loud voice. He threw himself at Jesus' feet. He let gratitude become his posture.

And Jesus, seeing more than his clean skin, saw his clean soul.

"Thy faith hath made thee whole."

Wholeness Over Healing

Whole.

Not just healed. Whole.

There's a word for that in the Greek: *sozo*. It means to save. To deliver. To restore. It speaks not just of external wellness but of inner transformation.

Nine walked away with changed skin. One walked away with a changed soul.

This moment wasn't just about a miracle—it was a preview of redemption. A glimpse of what Jesus came to do: not merely to cleanse skin but to restore hearts. Not just to give health, but to give salvation.

A Story That Looks Like Us

This passage is more than a footnote on gratitude. It is a mirror held up to every heart that has ever received more than it returned.

We are all the nine.

We've all walked away from answered prayers without a word.

We've all basked in blessings and failed to bless the One who gave them. We've all stood at the edge of mercy and forgotten to kneel.

But we can also be the one.

We can turn around. We can remember. We can run to the feet of the Savior and say—loudly, humbly, joyfully—"Thank you."

We can glorify God not just with our songs, but with our lives.

Gratitude, after all, is not just an emotion. It's a decision. A direction. A discipline.

It chooses to turn around.

It refuses to be swept away by the momentum of gain.

It acknowledges that the Giver matters more than the gift.

And when we walk that road—when we become the one rather than the nine—we discover something more profound than answered prayer. We discover the presence of Jesus.

The One Who Came Back: A Modern Reflection

A woman once told me her story. Years of addiction, darkness, and loss. A rehab program introduced her to Christ. She got clean. Got a job. Got her family back. And for a while, she forgot.

Until one day, in a church service, they sang "Amazing Grace." Something broke. She ran to the altar—years later—and wept. "I never thanked Him," she said. "I never really thanked Him."

That was the day she turned around. Not to be cleansed—but to be made whole.

————————— • ♦ • —————————

The Answer Asks You...

- Have I thanked Jesus for what He's done—or have I just moved on?
- Am I chasing the gift or seeking the Giver?
- In what ways might I be one of the nine today?
- What would it look like for me to turn around—to worship with my whole heart?
- Has my faith made me whole, or have I settled for being merely clean?

CHAPTER FOUR

The Question of Loyalty When the Crowd Walks Away

"Then said Jesus unto the twelve, Will ye also go away?"
—JOHN 6:67

• ◆ •

The sun was still warm on the Galilean hillside when they first followed Him. Full stomachs, hopeful hearts, dreams of deliverance. But by day's end, the crowd had thinned—and the question remained. In one conversation, Jesus sifted followers from fans, turning multiplication into a moment of decision.

What They Wanted vs. What He Offered

It began with a miracle. Five loaves. Two fish. A multitude fed. To the crowd, it was more than provision—it was proof. This must be the Prophet Moses had foretold, the King who could overthrow Rome, the Provider who would satisfy every need. They surged with expectation. "Make Him King," they whispered.

But Jesus withdrew. He had not come to be crowned by convenience. He had come to redeem—and the two were not the same.

The next morning, they found Him again. But He saw through their curiosity. "Ye seek me," He said, "not because ye saw the miracles, but because ye did eat of the loaves, and were filled." He wasn't fooled by their enthusiasm, and He wouldn't feed their misconceptions. Instead of giving them what they craved, He offered what they needed.

And what a message it was: "I am the Bread of Life... Except ye eat the flesh of the Son of Man, and drink his blood, ye have no life in you." The synagogue grew quiet. The people blinked. Their brows furrowed. Was He suggesting something unlawful, even cannibalistic? The metaphor was spiritual, but their minds were carnal. Their messianic expectations shattered under the weight of a message that was not about national deliverance but personal surrender.

When the Message Is Too Much

Even His disciples whispered, "This is a hard saying; who can hear it?" Jesus could have softened the metaphor or clarified His intent. He could have gathered them for an explanation, offered context, or reassured their confusion. But He didn't. He turned the dial even higher.

"Doth this offend you?" He asked. Then, in a voice full of grace and truth, He added, "The words that I speak unto you, they are spirit, and they are life."

Many would not receive them. They walked away—not just spectators, but those who had once followed closely. Scripture records that they "walked no more with him." Not for a season. Not for a sabbatical. They were gone.

And Jesus let them go. He never chased the crowd. He never changed the message to make it more palatable.

When the Question Comes for You

Then Jesus turned to the twelve. He turned—not to the crowd, but to the committed. The miracle workers. The close friends. The ones who had seen Him laugh and bleed.

It's one of the most vulnerable moments in the Gospels. He who was fully divine was also fully human, and though He needed nothing from man, He longed for their loyalty.

His question pierced the stillness: "Will ye also go away?"

This was not a rhetorical question, nor was it theatrical. It was intimate. Personal. Weighty.

It still is.

What do you do when the words of Christ shake you more than they settle you? When the Savior you followed for provision now calls you to crucifixion? When His truth wounds before it heals?

Trust in Tension

Peter spoke for the group, and perhaps, for all who have ever struggled to stay when leaving seems easier. "Lord, to whom shall we go? Thou hast the words of eternal life."

He didn't say, "We understand." He didn't say, "We like this plan." He admitted, "We have nowhere else to go." It was not a cry of triumph but a sigh of surrender. A tired, trembling declaration that, despite the confusion, Jesus was still the One they trusted.

That is the essence of discipleship: not comfort, but conviction; not clarity, but commitment. Peter knew the teaching was hard, but he also knew the Teacher. He trusted the One who spoke, even when the words were unsettling.

When Others Quietly Walk Away

Still today, many walk away—not always in loud rebellion, but often in quiet reorientation. They slip out, not through the church door, but in their hearts. The change is not always declared, but it is discernible in priorities, affections, and allegiances.

Sociologists now call this group the "nones"—those who claim no religious affiliation. In the early 1990s, they made up just

8% of the U.S. population. Today, that number exceeds 30% and climbs higher among younger generations, according to data from the Pew Research Center's 2021 report on the decline of Christianity in America (*Pew Research Center, December 14, 2021*).

Ken Ham's book *Gone* highlights another sobering trend: two-thirds of young adults who regularly attended church as children now leave by their twenties—and most never return. Many cite disillusionment, intellectual doubts, or a sense that the church doesn't matter anymore.

They didn't storm out. They faded. Not with anger, but with apathy. Not with heresy, but with hunger left unmet.

What did they want? A Jesus who inspires, not one who offends. A gospel of affirmation, not transformation. A Savior who multiplies bread, but not one who divides truth.

But the real Jesus does both.

He multiplies grace—and He multiplies expectations. He divides the faithful from the fickle—not by force, but by truth. He calls us not just to believe in Him, but to abide in Him, even when the abiding is costly.

Stay When the Message Is Hard

"Love your enemies."
"Deny yourself."
"Take up your cross."

"Forgive seventy times seven."
"Go and sin no more."

These are not words for the crowd. These are words for the called. They challenge, convict, and change us. And for those who remain—for those who, like Peter, say yes despite not understanding—they become words of life.

Jesus doesn't require you to comprehend everything He says, but He does call you to trust the One who speaks.
And that is enough.

A Whispered Commitment

You won't always like what Jesus says. But if you know Him— if you've seen His kindness in your worst moment, His mercy in your failure, and His power in your weakness—then you know there is nowhere else to go.

Let others chase miracles without the Man. Let others redefine truth to fit their story. Let others walk away.

We will stay.
We will stay when the sermon is hard, when the culture shifts, and when faith feels fragile. Not because we are strong, but because we are His. Because His words have marked us. And because, even when we don't understand the way, we trust the One who is the Way.

He asks you the same. And when the silence settles, may your answer echo Peter's:

"To whom shall we go?"

Because no one speaks like Jesus.
No one loves like Jesus.
And no one stays like Jesus.

———————————————— • ◆ • ————————————————

The Answer asks you...

- Have you ever found yourself drifting from Christ—not in body, but in heart, attention, or affection?
- What "hard sayings" of Jesus challenge you the most right now?
- How do you respond when the truth of Christ confronts your expectations or lifestyle?
- In what ways do your priorities reveal whether you are staying with Jesus or walking away?
- If Jesus asked you today, "Will you also go away?"—how would you answer?

CHAPTER FIVE

The Question of Trust during Storms

"And he said unto them, Why are ye so fearful?
How is it that ye have no faith?"
—MARK 4:40

———————— • ◆ • ————————

The sun had set on a long day of ministry. Jesus, worn from
the crowds, stepped into the boat with His disciples. What
followed wasn't just a journey across a lake—it was a revelation
that would shake their assumptions, then still their hearts.

When the Storm Finds You in Obedience

It began as a routine crossing. Familiar waters. Trusted hands.
The disciples, many of them seasoned fishermen, launched the
boat with practiced ease. Jesus had spoken: "Let us go to the
other side." They obeyed, likely without hesitation. It wasn't
their first trip. But it would be their most unforgettable one.

The Sea of Galilee is a paradox—peaceful in appearance, yet prone to violent, sudden winds that tumble down from the surrounding hills. That night, the wind didn't just stir; it roared. Waves began to rise with unexpected fury, slapping the boat and swallowing its edges. The vessel heaved and tilted. Water splashed in. Men scrambled.

And where was Jesus?

He was sleeping.

Not meditating. Not pacing. Not watching. Sleeping.

What a picture—humanity wrapped in exhaustion, curled on a cushion in the stern of a storm-tossed boat. He had healed the sick that day, touched the untouchables, preached to crowds. Now, He slept with the deep weariness only the truly human can feel.

And yet—this sleeping man would soon speak, and creation would fall silent.

That contrast—the slumber of man and the authority of God—anchors this moment in sacred mystery.

When Faith Cries Out Through Fear

In panic, the disciples woke Him. Their cry was unpolished, urgent:

"Lord, save us: we perish."

It was faith wrapped in fear. The address—"Lord"—showed reverence. The plea—"save us"—expressed hope. But the confession—"we perish"—revealed raw terror.

They didn't recite a psalm. They didn't rehearse a doctrinal statement. They gasped out the truth. And sometimes, that's enough.

Jesus stood up.
No thunder of introduction. No dramatic buildup. He rose—not merely from slumber, but into His sovereignty. He spoke—not to the disciples, but to the elements.

"Peace. Be still."
Or literally, "Be quiet. Be muzzled."

The wind obeyed. The waves flattened. The chaos collapsed into calm.

It didn't taper off—it stopped. Suddenly. Utterly.

The disciples were drenched in silence now—awash not in seawater but in awe. And Jesus, the one who moments earlier had dozed like a worn-out traveler, now stood with the commanding presence of the Creator.

The storm didn't wake Him. Their voices did.

And then came His question:

"Why are you fearful, O ye of little faith?"

It wasn't mockery. It wasn't scorn. It was a mirror.

Why fear, when I am with you?
Why tremble, when I'm not trembling?
Why doubt, when I have never failed?

Fear isn't just an emotion—it's a theology. It reveals what we believe about God. And faith, even mustard-seed small, displaces fear when it's rightly placed in the One who sleeps not out of indifference but because He's already in control.

Faith Beyond the Shore

This boat ride wasn't an accident. It was an assignment. Jesus didn't lead them around the storm—He led them into it.

That's discipleship. It's not the avoidance of hardship but the presence of Christ in hardship.

When you follow Jesus, you're saying yes to more than a safe commute. You're saying yes to purpose, presence, and sometimes, pressure.

Jesus was teaching them more than how to travel. He was teaching them who to trust.

How easy it is to trust what feels familiar. The boat. The sail. The stars. The shoreline.

What we often call "faith" is just comfort disguised. We feel secure because we've done this before. But true faith begins where our control ends.

QUESTIONS FROM THE ANSWER

Jesus allowed the storm to shake the boat so He could reveal who truly steadies it.

When God unsettles your comfort zone, it's not to sink you—but to show you that your anchor has a name.

When the Storm Is More Than Weather

Not every storm is a spiritual assault—but some are.

This one was. On the other side of the lake, Jesus would confront demoniacs—men bound by forces of darkness. Satan wasn't ignorant of that. So, he stirred the waters to resist the crossing.

When God's purpose is advancing, resistance often intensifies.

Sometimes, the turbulence isn't random—it's targeted. The enemy trembles when you're near a breakthrough.

In those moments, what do you do?

Draw near. That's what the disciples did. They "came to" Jesus, not just geographically, but spiritually. They leaned into Him—not away.

Trouble has a way of locating your trust. And storms don't just shake boats—they reveal foundations.

Like a child running into their parent's bed during thunder, we're wired to run to someone bigger when we're afraid.

It's in the shaking that we remember: we're not built to weather storms alone.

Then—call out. Not with polish. Not with posture. Just honesty.

"Lord, save us."

Five words. That's all it took.

No preamble. No eloquence. Just desperation wrapped in belief.

God doesn't grade prayers on grammar—He responds to the heart.

When Christ Stands, Calm Comes

Two words dominated that night: tempest and calm.

The storm had a personality—boisterous, violent, untamed. But when Jesus rose, so did peace.

One "arose" to destroy.
The other "arose" to deliver.

That's the difference between human fear and divine power. Fear tries to swallow us. Christ stands to save us.

Notice His demeanor before the miracle. He wasn't just present—He was resting.

That's no small thing. It's easy to rest on a quiet shore. But Jesus rested on a rising sea.

Why?

Because He wasn't governed by what surrounded Him—He was grounded in what sustained Him.

He slept as man—but spoke as God.

No one else can claim that.

His humanity let Him share our frailty. His divinity let Him calm our fears.

We often think power looks like action. But in Jesus, power sometimes looks like rest—secure, still, unmoved by the chaos around.

It reminds me of what a seasoned pilot once said about turbulence: "While the passengers are gripping their armrests, the cockpit is calm."

That's Jesus in the storm. While we panic, He is perfectly composed.

Not because He doesn't care—but because He's already in control.

When Fear Shifts to Awe

Some storms are not detours. They are discipleship.

When Jesus speaks, nature listens. Wind halts. Waves hush. The sea, wild and thrashing, becomes like glass.

And the disciples? They marvel.

They don't high-five. They don't cheer. They stare.

"What manner of man is this, that even the winds and the sea obey him?"

The kind who sleeps like us, but speaks like no one else.

And something deeper happened in that moment. Their fear shifted. No longer were they afraid of the storm—now they were in awe of the One who silenced it.

The lesson was more than meteorological—it was theological.

They had feared the waves. Now, they feared the Word.

It's one thing to tremble at what threatens your life. It's another to tremble before the One who gives you life.

When the Storms Are Yours

For college students, storms may look like pressure to perform, loneliness in a crowd, unexpected financial strain, or the ache of spiritual doubt.

For pastors, it might be the quiet pain of leadership fatigue, the burden of unmet expectations, or the heartbreak of ministry betrayal.

Whatever the boat, whatever the storm—Jesus is still there.

And His power wasn't just displayed to impress; it was given to comfort.

He stands, so you don't have to sink.

You are not alone in the storm.
And when the waves rise, ask again—*Why are you afraid?*

———————— • ◆ • ————————

The Answer asks you...

- What does Jesus' rest in the middle of the storm reveal about the kind of peace He offers you personally?
- Where have you mistaken familiarity or routine for actual dependence on Christ?
- How do you typically respond when fear creeps in—by drawing nearer to Jesus or drifting toward panic?
- Is there a current storm you're facing that might be an assignment rather than an accident? How might Jesus be present in it?
- Have you ever seen Jesus calm a storm in your life—emotionally, spiritually, or circumstantially? What did that reveal about who He is?

CHAPTER SIX

The Question of Judgment and Self-Examination

"And why beholdest thou the mote that is in
thy brother's eye, but perceivest not the beam
that is in thine own eye?"

—LUKE 6:41

———————— • ◆ • ————————

The mountainside was quiet, but His words thundered. In the
hush of the Sermon on the Mount, Jesus wasn't raising His
voice—He was raising hearts. He was pulling back the curtain
on spiritual life, inviting His listeners to trade self-righteousness
for self-awareness, to stop pointing and start seeing.

The Mirror and the Window

Some questions shake the soul, not because they're loud—but
because they're true. Jesus didn't thunder. He didn't accuse. He

simply asked: "Why are you so focused on the tiny flaw in your brother's life, while ignoring the glaring issue in your own?"

Picture it: two men, face to face. One squinting through the window at a speck in his brother's eye—maybe just a fleck of sawdust. The other, oblivious to the beam jutting from his own eye like a floor joist in plain sight. As a picture, it's absurd. But as a reflection, it's painfully accurate. That's what hypocrisy looks like when heaven hands us a mirror.

The problem is, we prefer windows to mirrors. Windows let us watch others. Mirrors make us face ourselves. Windows feed our assumptions; mirrors demand our repentance. And if we're not careful, we'll spend our lives peering outward—while the real work of grace waits on the other side of the glass.

We love mirrors... as long as we're not the ones standing in front of them.

The Danger of a Critical Spirit

We're fluent in the flaws of others. "He's bitter." "She's fake." "They're just performing." We have categories. Labels. Hashtags. But Jesus doesn't ask, *"Why is there a speck?"* He asks, *"Why do you see it?"*

It's a question about gaze. About attention. Why is it so easy to spot someone else's stumble, and so hard to sense your own pride?

Blind Spots and Beams

Here's the paradox: The more pride grows, the more perception shrinks.

Spiritual beams are deceptive because they impair our vision without our consent. You can't see clearly when arrogance clouds your sight. You become suspicious instead of sensitive. Harsh instead of holy. Judgmental instead of just.

Jesus doesn't outlaw discernment. He establishes order: "First, remove the beam from your own eye. Then you'll see clearly…" Correction without confession is contamination. You can't help heal someone when you're infected with spiritual superiority.

Soft Eyes, Washed Hands

Like a surgeon, before he takes the scalpel, your soul must be scrubbed in humility. You speak truth best when it's carried in hands that tremble with mercy.

The Church has too often been known for its gavel, not its grace. For the thud of judgment, not the balm of compassion. But the early Church didn't carry stones—they carried scars. They didn't hurl rebukes—they held hands.

Grace makes you gentle. Forgiveness makes you kind. Holiness makes you humble.

Measure for Measure

Jesus warns us, "With what judgment ye judge, ye shall be judged." It's not karma—it's character. Heaven watches the ruler you use. And sometimes, it wraps back around.

Bitter eyes see bitterness. Harsh hearts assume harm. But grace-laced souls? They see beauty. Possibility. Redemption.

Here's the strange math of the gospel: the more honest you are about your own beam, the more gently you'll touch someone else's speck.

The Hypocrite's Pretense

In verse 5, Jesus uses the word "hypocrite." In His day, the term referred to actors in Greek theater—those who wore masks to play roles. It wasn't just about dishonesty; it was about duality. Pretending. Performing. Wearing the mask of holiness without the heart of it.

And Jesus was especially direct with those who wore the robes of religion while harboring contempt. The Pharisees were experts at law—but novices at love.

But the antidote to pretense isn't performance—it's repentance. And when repentance comes, it never arrives quietly.

The Revival of Repentance

I once heard of a revival that didn't begin with a sermon—but with a sentence.

A man stood and said, "I'm the one who needs to repent." That was all. No spotlight. No stagecraft. Just an honest confession from a humbled heart. And something shifted. You could feel it in the room—like a dam giving way, like a burden finally falling off weary shoulders.

It wasn't eloquence that stirred the crowd. It wasn't emotion. It was honesty. Humility broke the silence—and grace rushed in.

People didn't rush to critique—they rushed to confess. There were no accusers left, only worshipers. Because that's what happens when we finally see the beam—not as a mark of shame, but as the beginning of healing.

Not a wall that disqualifies us—but a window into our own need for grace. And from that place of repentance, we're able to speak truth—not with pride, but with mercy.

A Modern Speck and Beam

Imagine this: A church member posts a vague, critical comment online. "Some people need to get their hearts right before serving on stage." Dozens like the post. Some know exactly who it's about.

But what if, instead of posting, they had paused? What if they had asked, "Is there something in my eye?" What if they had sent a message—not to accuse, but to ask, "Are you okay? Can I pray with you?"

The difference between condemnation and compassion is often just one beam away.

The Wisdom of the Wounded

Those who've carried beams in their own eyes speak differently. They've been humbled. Softened. Sanctified.

They remember what it's like to limp.

Jesus, the Carpenter, knew wood. He shaped it. Smoothed it. Carried it.

And one day, He stretched across it. Not just a beam—but a cross.

So maybe the question isn't just, "Why do you see the speck?" Maybe it's, "Why do you ignore the cross?"

Because when you see the Cross, you stop throwing hammers. You start holding grace.

The Church's Calling

This isn't just a personal word—it's a corporate one.

What if the Church became known not as the place where people are misjudged but where they're truly met?

What if we traded assumptions for empathy, silence for listening, and judgment for grace?

What if we stopped shouting through windows—and dared to face the mirror?

What if we spent less time calling out the world—and more time letting God call out what's in us?

The Final Invitation

The mirror still stands. The question still echoes.

"And why beholdest thou the mote that is in thy brother's eye, but considerest not the beam that is in thine own eye?"

It's not just a question about judgment. It's a question about Jesus. Because underneath the splinters and beams, the critique and confession, stands the Carpenter—the One who sees clearly, heals completely, and loves fully.

He asks not to accuse, but to awaken. He holds up the mirror not to shame us, but to show us Himself. Because the one who asks this question is not just our teacher—He is our Savior. The only One with no speck, no beam, no sin. And yet He bore ours. Carried them. Nailed them to a cross He didn't deserve.

Why? Because Jesus is not just the One asking the question. He is the Answer to it.

He is the answer to our blindness—offering sight.

The answer to our pride—offering grace.
The answer to our judgment—offering mercy.
The answer to our sin—offering salvation.

Every question He asks leads back to who He is. Every mirror He holds up reflects His heart. A heart full of truth. Full of tenderness. Full of healing.

So when you hear Him ask, *"Why do you see the speck?"*—listen closely. It's not condemnation. It's invitation. An invitation to come to the One who sees you as you are and loves you still. The One who removes beams, restores vision, and renews the soul.

Jesus is the Answer. To this question. To every question.

And He's waiting—mirror in hand, arms open wide.

———————— • ◆ • ————————

The Answer Asks You...

- When have you been quick to point out someone's speck, while ignoring your own beam?
- How does the idea of "soft eyes" challenge the way you speak about others—especially online?
- What would it look like to examine your own heart before offering correction to someone else?
- How might Jesus' use of the word "hypocrite" apply to modern-day religious attitudes?
- What beam are you asking God to help you remove today?

CHAPTER SEVEN

The Question of Faith That Reaches in Desperation

"And Jesus said, Who touched me? When all denied, Peter and they that were with him said, Master, the multitude throng thee and press thee, and sayest thou, Who touched me?"
—LUKE 8:45

———————— • ◆ • ————————

Jesus had just crossed the Sea of Galilee, returning to Capernaum. A crowd was already waiting on the shore. As He stepped out of the boat, Jairus—a respected synagogue leader—fell at His feet and pleaded with Him to come. His daughter was dying. Time was short. Jesus agreed, and together they moved through the narrow streets, the crowd swelling around them, eager, urgent, electric with hope.

But amid the noise and movement, another story was unfolding—quieter, hidden in the fringe. A woman, unnamed and long unseen, slipped through the crowd. Not to speak. Not to be noticed. But simply to reach.

Twelve Years of Silence

The street pulsed with expectation. People leaned in from every side—dust on their feet, sweat on their brows, hope in their eyes. Mothers hoisted children onto their hips. The old clutched worn staffs. The young surged forward, jostling for a better view. Jesus was walking with Jairus. A ruler's daughter was dying, and heaven itself seemed on the move. But just behind them, trailing from the shadows, came another kind of desperation. One without rank or status. One without a name.

She had lived twelve years in silence. Not the peaceful kind, but the kind that isolates. Her body had betrayed her. A slow, persistent issue of blood that refused to stop. Doctors had poked and prodded, remedies had failed, coins had run out, and hope had thinned like the edges of her shawl.

For twelve years she had not been touched. Not with affection. Not with welcome. She was unclean, labeled by the law, cast outside the margins of worship and community. Every bed she sat on, every seat she touched, was defiled. People avoided her with the same instinct they avoided corpses.

But she had heard of Jesus.

One Touch of Faith

The stories whispered into alleyways and down corridors. He opened the eyes of the blind. He drove out demons. He spoke to lepers. He touched the untouchables. She didn't need Him to stop—just to pass close enough for one touch. If she could just get close—close enough to brush the edge of His robe.

She pushed into the crowd like someone swimming upstream. Every step was a risk. Every movement carried the potential for rejection, discovery, shame.

And then, in a moment of courage born of desperation, she reached forward and touched the hem of His garment.

No one saw it. Not at first. But she felt it. Instantly. The bleeding stopped. Her strength returned. It was as if the storm inside her had been calmed by a single note of peace.

A Savior Who Stops

As Jairus stood in urgent silence, hope paused.
Because Jesus stopped—for someone else.
The crowd halted. And Jesus asked, "Who touched me?"

The words fell like a ripple over water. Peter, ever the realist, was quick to respond. "Master, the multitude throng thee and press thee, and sayest thou, Who touched me?"

But Jesus didn't smile at Peter's logic. He looked beyond it.

"Somebody hath touched me: for I perceive that virtue is gone out of me."

The woman's heart must have dropped. She hadn't meant to cause a scene. She didn't want a spotlight—she wanted to disappear into her healing. But the One she touched wasn't a magician performing tricks for crowds. He was a Shepherd seeking the sheep that reached for Him.

Twelve voices warred inside her—run, hide, disappear. The same voices that had kept her in the shadows for twelve years. But for the first time, another voice spoke louder: You're healed. And He is calling you forward.

Trembling, she stepped forward. She fell at His feet and told her story. The whole story. The pain, the shame, the years of being unseen, the risk she took, the healing she now felt pulsing through her body.

The Word That Changed Everything

And then came the word that changed her life.

"Daughter."

The crowd likely gasped. Maybe the woman did too.

"Daughter."

It was the only time Jesus ever used that word to address someone directly in all the Gospel accounts. He could have said "woman," as He had with others. He could have referred to her generically. But He didn't. He spoke a word that reached into the hollowness of her isolation and filled it with belonging.

"Daughter."

A word she hadn't heard in years—if ever. Maybe her own family had turned away when her illness persisted. Maybe the synagogue had stopped calling her name. Maybe neighbors no longer greeted her in the market. For twelve long years, her identity had been slowly stripped away, not just by the sickness in her body, but by the silence that followed her everywhere she went. She wasn't just bleeding—she was forgotten.

Until Jesus spoke.

In one word, He restored what the world had taken. In one word, He claimed her. Not as a nuisance. Not as a problem. Not as a risk to His reputation.

But as a daughter.

"Be of good comfort," He continued. "Thy faith hath made thee whole; go in peace."

She had hoped for healing—but she received more than that. She was not merely cured. She was welcomed. Affirmed. Cherished. Whole—not just in her body, but in her soul. Not just cleansed, but claimed.

Faith That Cannot Hide

We never learn her name. But we learn what heaven calls her.

She had been hidden in the crowd, but now she stood at the center of Jesus' gaze. She had been unclean for over a decade, and now she was embraced into the family of God with one word. One act of faith. One touch.

It wasn't the crowd that moved Him. It wasn't proximity. It was faith.

Do you see it? Do you feel it?

We serve a Savior who distinguishes the accidental from the intentional. Who knows the difference between casual contact and desperate faith? Who but Jesus would notice the unseen, feel the quiver of a reaching hand—and stop all of heaven's movement to meet her there?

"Who touched me?" That question was not born of confusion. Jesus knew exactly who had reached out. But He asked because He wanted her to know something too—that she was not invisible. Not anonymous. Not forgotten.

He wanted her to hear what the crowd never would have said: You are mine. You are seen. You are safe.

He asked not to shame her, but to name her. To call her something the world never had: beloved. To call her what God had always known her to be: daughter.

A High Priest Who Feels

She hadn't just touched His robe—she'd touched His heart. Because this High Priest isn't distant. He's familiar with the ache. Hebrews says He's "touched with the feeling of our infirmities." It's not theology on a scroll. It's the look in His eyes when He said, "Daughter."

That word—touched—in the Greek is *sumpatheō*. It's where we get our word "sympathy." But it means more than polite empathy. It means to feel with. To share the burden. To step into the ache.

Jesus does not observe our suffering from a distance. He enters it. He doesn't merely witness our heartbreak—He carries it. He doesn't offer comfort like a stranger. He offers it like someone who has bled too.

When that woman reached for the hem of His garment, she was reaching for healing. But Jesus was reaching for her. His power flowed out, yes—but more than that, His heart turned toward her. He did not recoil from her uncleanness. He did not flinch at her hidden shame. He welcomed it. He honored it. He called her forward not just to heal her body but to touch her soul.

That is what our High Priest does. He doesn't brush past us in the crowd. He stops for us. He doesn't merely wave a hand and move on. He kneels to see us eye to eye.

He enters the mess of our lives—not as a visitor, but as One who understands it from the inside. Betrayal? He felt it.

Weariness? He knew it. Rejection? He bore it. Fear, sorrow, tears, hunger, grief—He has walked every road you walk.

He is still the Christ who stops everything when one hurting soul dares to reach. He is still the Savior who asks, "Who touched me?"—not because He doesn't know, but because He wants you to know that He sees. He feels. He cares.

And when you finally come forward, trembling with the truth of your story, He will not scold you. He will not shame you.

The Answer to your need will speak your name. And if you listen closely, you might even hear Him say it again:

"Daughter."

The Answer Asks You...

- Where in your life have you felt unseen, unnamed, or forgotten?
- What would it look like for you to reach out to Jesus in quiet desperation?
- Have you ever tried to disappear into healing— avoiding deeper restoration?
- Do you believe Jesus sees *you* in the crowd?
- What name might Jesus be speaking over your shame today?

CHAPTER EIGHT

The Question of Worry and God's Daily Provision

"Which of you by taking thought can add one
cubit unto his stature?"
—MATTHEW 6:27

———————— • ◆ • ————————

It's no secret—we are anxious people.

Turn on the news. Scroll through your phone. Glance around
a crowded room. You'll see it written in the slump of our
shoulders, the furrow in our brows, the buzz beneath our
conversations. Anxiety isn't just a passing emotion anymore—
it's a way of life.

We worry about inflation and identity theft, about our
children's education and our own relevance. We fret about the
things we can't control, and we try to control them anyway.
The irony? We are the most medicated, most counseled, and
most technologically equipped generation in history, and yet,

according to global research, Americans are among the most anxious people on earth.

Long before anxiety became a diagnosis, it was already a concern of the heart. Jesus addressed it not in a clinic, but on a hillside.

And then He asked a question. Not a scolding or a solution. A question that still echoes through the anxious noise:

"Which of you by taking thought can add one cubit unto his stature?"

In other words: Has worry ever made you taller? Has anxiety ever solved your problem?

He's not condemning us—He's calling us. This is no rhetorical jab. It's a Savior's whisper in a world gone frantic: *You don't have to live this way.*

The Master of Gentle Questions

Jesus could have thundered. He could have barked commands and demanded peace. But instead, He asked questions.

Not to accuse, but to awaken. His were not the inquiries of a prosecutor—they were the invitations of a Shepherd. This quiet question about worry does what no lecture ever could: it draws our eyes from the mirror of self to the face of God.

Is Not the Life More?

The sun is warm on the Galilean hillside. A crowd listens as Jesus begins to teach—not with rebuke, but with wonder:

"Is not the life more than meat, and the body than raiment?"

He's not dismissing our needs. He's reminding us of our value. You are more than your job. More than your bank account. More than your performance or productivity.

Life is more. And the One who breathed life into you knows exactly what you need.

A Sermon in Flight

"Behold the fowls of the air..."

Jesus points skyward. A sparrow flits past. A lark dives for seed. "Watch them," He says.

They don't plant. They don't harvest. Yet they eat. Every single day. Not because they earned it—but because God gave it.

A few months ago, I was in a quiet church before the congregation gathered. The sanctuary was still. No music. No crowd. Just silence and sunbeams filtering through stained glass. Then I heard it—a flutter overhead. A small bird had somehow found its way in, circling the balcony before gliding down toward the front. It paused for a moment on the pulpit, then lifted off again, wings brushing the air as it flew toward the steeple windows.

And in that moment, it struck me: even the bird was preaching. Not with words—but with trust.

What if we lived that way? Not recklessly—but confidently. What if we believed Jesus when He said, "Are ye not much better than they?"

A Sermon in Stillness

Then Jesus shifts the scene again.

"Consider the lilies of the field, how they grow..."

Lilies don't wake up in panic. They don't measure or spin. They simply grow. They unfold in beauty, fully trusting the God who clothed them.

"Even Solomon in all his glory was not arrayed like one of these."

If God adorns perishable petals, how much more does He care for those He's redeemed?

Jesus' words now cut gently but firmly:

"O ye of little faith."

That's what worry reveals. Not a lack of time. Not a resource shortage. A crisis of trust.

The False Productivity of Worry

Worry feels responsible. It masquerades as action. It tells us we're being mature, engaged, in control.

But Jesus tells us the truth: worry is not harmless. It is misplaced belief.

Oswald Chambers said it plainly:

"All our fret and worry is caused by calculating without God." Worry is not just anxiety—it is accidental atheism. It is life lived as though God is absent.

The Kingdom First, the Rest Follows

At the center of Jesus' teaching is this famous declaration:

"But seek ye first the kingdom of God, and his righteousness; and all these things shall be added unto you." *(v. 33)*

This is not a cosmic vending machine formula. It's an invitation to reorder our loves.

If you fill your life with trivial things first, the important things won't fit. But if you begin with God—His kingdom, His righteousness—everything else finds its place.

He's not promising ease. He's offering alignment.

Living in Today's Grace

"Take therefore no thought for the morrow..."

Jesus isn't advocating for carelessness. He's calling for trust. You don't have grace for tomorrow yet. You have grace for *today*. Trying to hoard strength for the future only depletes the strength you need now.

Corrie ten Boom knew this deeply. She once said:

"Worry does not empty tomorrow of its sorrow. It empties today of its strength."

God's grace is not given in bulk. It's given fresh. Like manna. Like morning light.

The Question That Calms

Let's return to the question: *"Which of you by taking thought can add one cubit unto his stature?"* What has worry ever added? It subtracts—peace, rest, joy. But God adds. He adds peace that passes understanding, strength for the day, and beauty in the waiting. When we fix our gaze on Him, anxiety begins to loosen its grip.

Daily Trust, Daily Grace

Think again of that bird in the sanctuary. It didn't panic. It didn't plan its escape. It simply flew—drawn to the light, trusting the air beneath its wings. It didn't know where the opening was, but it knew how to move. That's the invitation Jesus gives us. Not to solve tomorrow. Not to map out every outcome. But to trust Him today.

He never promised a life without needs. But He did promise that our Father knows them. He never guaranteed tomorrow's clarity. But He did promise today's grace. And that changes everything. Not because we know what's coming—but because we know who's providing.

———————— • ◆ • ————————

The Answer Asks You...

- What worries have you been carrying alone that God never asked you to hold?
- In what ways has worry subtly become your false sense of control?
- What would it look like for you to seek God's kingdom first—today?
- Where in your life do you see God already providing, as He does for birds and lilies?
- What is one anxiety you can write down and surrender to Jesus in prayer?

CHAPTER NINE

The Question of Hope in the Face of Death

"And whosoever liveth and believeth in me shall never die. Believest thou this?"
—JOHN 11:26

— • ◆ • —

They sent word quickly. Time was running out.

"Lord, behold, he whom thou lovest is sick."

No demands. No desperate plea. Just a message wrapped in trust. The one You love is sick.

The subtext was clear enough: You'll come, won't You? Because that's what love does. It doesn't delay when breath is shallow. It doesn't hesitate when death is near.

But Jesus didn't rush. He didn't flinch. He didn't rearrange His schedule or gather His things in a panic. Instead, He stayed. Two more days in the same place.

Two days of silence. Two days of waiting. Two days that must have felt like two eternities in Bethany.

In that house filled with shadows and uncertainty, Mary and Martha must have watched the road with straining eyes— hoping to see the silhouette of their Healer in the distance. He healed strangers, after all. Surely He would hurry for a friend.

But the road stayed empty. And their brother stopped breathing.

When Hope Feels Late

By the time Jesus arrived, Lazarus had been in the tomb for four days. The grieving had shifted from shock to sorrow. Death had settled in. Cold. Final. Undeniable.

Martha, always the first to speak, came out to meet Him. But there was no embrace. Her words carried the ache of both faith and frustration.

"Lord, if thou hadst been here, my brother had not died."

It wasn't only disappointment. It was faith mixed with heartache. She had seen what Jesus could do—had no doubt He had the power to intervene. That's what made the waiting so painful. He could have come. But He didn't.

Still, even in the heaviness of that moment, something stirred. A faint, stubborn hope rose through the sorrow.

"But I know, that even now, whatsoever thou wilt ask of God, God will give it thee."

She wasn't sure what that meant. She only knew who He was. And that knowing was enough to keep her leaning forward, even when everything inside her wanted to fall apart.

Jesus looked at her—not with rebuke, but with a promise.

"Thy brother shall rise again."

Martha reached for what she had been taught.

"I know that he shall rise again in the resurrection at the last day."

It was the comfort of good theology—hope deferred, someday comfort. It was true—but not near enough. Jesus wasn't pointing to a day. He was pointing to Himself.

"I am the resurrection, and the life: he that believeth in me, though he were dead, yet shall he live: And whosoever liveth and believeth in me shall never die."

Then came the question—the kind that doesn't echo across a crowd but lands in the soul.

"Believest thou this?"

When Truth Gets Personal

There is a kind of belief that's easy in the sanctuary and hard in the silence. It's one thing to believe Jesus is the Resurrection when you're healthy and the sun is shining. It's another when you're standing outside a tomb. When the prayer wasn't answered the way you hoped. When the silence stretched too long.

But Martha—bless her trembling, trusting heart—said yes.

"Yea, Lord: I believe that thou art the Christ, the Son of God, which should come into the world."

She didn't understand everything. But she trusted Someone. Faith, in its most beautiful form, is not certainty in an outcome. It's confidence in a Person.

The Savior Who Weeps

Mary came next. And though her words echoed her sister's— "Lord, if thou hadst been here, my brother had not died"—she brought more tears than theology.

She didn't try to reason her way through the grief. She simply collapsed in it.
And Jesus—God in flesh, King of creation, Commander of life and death—saw her.

And He wept.
He didn't preach. He didn't correct. He cried.

And not just a gentle tear. Scripture says He groaned—*embrimaomai*—a deep, guttural sorrow. The groan of a lion. The ache of a Creator standing before the brokenness of His creation.

He was not untouched by their pain. He felt it. Fully.

Love doesn't always speak—it sometimes breaks.

The God Who Groans Still

What kind of God does this? What kind of King delays the healing, walks into grief, and weeps before the miracle? The kind who knows that our greatest need is not just a solution—but a Savior who enters into our suffering.

When the Stone Stands Between

Jesus asked for the stone to be rolled away. Martha, practical as ever, hesitated. "Lord, by this time he stinketh: for he hath been dead four days."

Even faith flinches at the stench of death.

But Jesus gently reminded her:

"Said I not unto thee, that, if thou wouldest believe, thou shouldest see the glory of God?"

And they moved the stone.

Jesus didn't pray for power. He prayed so the people around Him would know where the power came from.

"Father, I thank thee that thou hast heard me."

Then He raised His voice—not in panic, but in authority.

"Lazarus, come forth."

And Lazarus did.

Wrapped in the grave clothes of yesterday's sorrow—but alive. Staggering into sunlight. Blinking at glory. Proof that the final word doesn't belong to death.

Lessons from Martha's Faith

There's something about Martha that lingers in this story. Not because she was perfect—but because she was honest.

She shows us that even faith with questions can be faith that pleases God. She teaches us that when our theology collides with our reality, we lean not into answers—but into Jesus. She reminds us that when Jesus delays, it's not divine forgetfulness. It's divine love in disguise.

That love doesn't always come in the form of immediate rescue. Sometimes, it comes as a presence in the waiting. As hope in the tomb. As resurrection after the fourth day.

What We Learn in the Waiting

Those days of silence before Jesus arrived in Bethany are not wasted space in the story.
They are where trust is forged.

Jesus could have arrived on day one. But He came on day four—when all human help had failed, when all natural hope was gone, when the body had begun to break down.

He came when *only God* could make a difference. And sometimes, that's when He comes to us, too.

A Question for Every Soul

"Believest thou this?"

The question isn't rhetorical. It's real. It's raw.

It's for every mother who's walked out of a NICU with empty arms.
Every father who's buried a dream.
Every widow who wakes to silence.
Every soul who wonders why Jesus didn't come sooner.

Do you believe that He's still good—even when the tomb is sealed?
Do you believe He's the resurrection—even when you haven't seen the miracle yet?
Do you believe He weeps with you—even when you feel alone?
Do you believe He is enough?

Because He is. He is the resurrection. He is the life. And He hasn't forgotten you.

He Still Calls the Dead to Life

The same voice that called Lazarus out of the grave still calls to you. Not just from death to life—but from despair to hope. From numbness to joy. From silence to song.

You may feel wrapped in grave clothes. You may think it's too late. But Jesus doesn't work on your timeline.

He works on His. And His timing, though mysterious, is always merciful.
Even now—especially now—He stands near.

Not with a lecture. Not with condemnation.
But with presence. With tears. With power.

The Answer is not only the One who raises the dead—but the One who stays when your world falls apart. The One who stands beside graves. And grief. And you.

And then, with gentleness, He asks:
Do you believe this?

—————————— • ◆ • ——————————

The Answer asks you...

- Do you believe Jesus sees your sorrow, even when He seems silent?
- Have you confused belief in an outcome with belief in a Person?
- What delays in your life might be divine invitations to deeper trust?
- How do you respond when faith collides with finality?
- Will you trust Jesus to show His glory—even when the tomb is sealed?

CHAPTER TEN

The Question of Prayer and Spiritual Watchfulness

"And he cometh unto the disciples, and findeth
them asleep, and saith unto Peter, What, could
ye not watch with me one hour?"
—MATTHEW 26:40

— • ♦ • —

They had never seen Him like this.

He had led them through storms and into villages teeming with
need. He had silenced Pharisees and stilled seas. He had broken
bread until it fed thousands, and broken silence until it fed the
soul. But now, in the shadows of Gethsemane, they saw
something altogether different. He was quiet. Heavy.
Unshakably burdened.

Gethsemane was familiar ground. John would later recall it was
a place "where Jesus ofttimes resorted." It was a favorite retreat,
an olive grove nestled on the Mount of Olives. But that night,

it wasn't restful. The air hung thick with something unspoken. The moon traced long shadows as the Master asked His disciples to do one thing—**watch with me.**

He took Peter, James, and John a little further into the grove, leaving the rest behind. These were His closest friends, the inner circle. They had seen Him transfigured in glory. They had heard the whispers of Moses and Elijah. And now He asked them to join Him—not in glory, but in grief.

"My soul is exceeding sorrowful, even unto death," He said. "Tarry ye here, and watch with me."

He went a little further. Fell to the ground. And prayed.

The Invitation to Intimacy: With Me One Hour

It's tempting to hear Christ's question—"What, could ye not watch with me one hour?"—as a harsh rebuke. But listen closely. It wasn't spoken like a scolding parent or a disappointed teacher. It was spoken like a friend. A hurting friend.

Jesus didn't ask for miracles. He didn't ask them to preach or fight or fix anything. He asked them to sit. To stay. To keep watch. Not over Him—but *with* Him. There's a difference.

The Greek word is *grēgoreō*—to remain awake, alert, attentive. But the phrase "with me" carries the real weight. This wasn't about staying up late. It was about standing near. Staying close. Entering into sorrow with someone you love.

Jesus, in the depths of His anguish, wasn't asking for help. He was requesting communion. The kind of communion that doesn't need words. The kind that comes when one friend simply sits beside another in the ache of a long night.

We live in a world of urgency—be there, do something, fix it now. But Jesus asked something far more tender: be with Me. Share the sorrow. Feel the weight. Watch—not for what's coming, but for *who's here.*

It was an invitation to intimacy. And they missed it.

The Failure of the Flesh: The Spirit Is Willing

When Jesus returned the first time, He found them asleep.

He had been sweating drops of blood. Agony had wrung His soul like a sponge. Heaven had received the most honest prayer ever uttered: "O my Father, if it be possible, let this cup pass from me: nevertheless not as I will, but as thou wilt." And the men He asked to stay awake—His brothers, His companions—were out cold.

There's no sarcasm in Jesus' voice. No fury. Just grief. Grief that in His greatest hour of need, He faced it alone. And then He said the words that sum up the frailty of the human heart:

"The spirit indeed is willing, but the flesh is weak."

They weren't wicked. They were weary.

Luke's Gospel adds a detail: they slept "for sorrow." That phrase catches in the throat. Sorrow had numbed them. All the talk of betrayal, denial, and death had pressed in on them like a storm cloud. And fatigue—the kind that comes from emotional overload—settled in. Their eyes closed, not from indifference, but from the heaviness of the moment.

But still... they slept.

And so do we. We sleep through sacred hours. We nap in the garden of presence. We close our eyes when our Lord asks us to keep them open.

Gethsemane doesn't condemn their failure. It reveals it. And in revealing theirs, it gently reflects ours. Because every believer at some point has meant to pray, and didn't. Meant to stay awake, and drifted off. Meant to stand, and stumbled.

The Hour of Decision: Sleep On Now

Jesus didn't give up on them. He went back to prayer. A second time. Then a third. The disciples? They kept sleeping.

And then the hour came. The moment shifted. The rustle of leaves wasn't just wind—it was footsteps. The glint of torchlight wasn't imagination—it was betrayal in motion.

Jesus turned and said something chillingly gentle:

"Sleep on now, and take your rest... behold, the hour is at hand."

Some hours cannot be reclaimed. Some invitations expire.

Judas was approaching. The soldiers were near. The garden, once still and private, now became a stage for treachery.

The disciples had missed their hour. Not in rebellion. In weariness. But missed nonetheless.

What Jesus offered them—one hour of sacred watching—was gone. Not with thunder. Not with punishment. Just with a question that echoes still:

Could you not watch with me?

The Grace of Restraint: Jesus Steps Forward

Watch what Jesus does next.

He doesn't roll His eyes. He doesn't say, "You're on your own now." He doesn't unchoose them.

He steps forward.

To Judas. To soldiers. To swords.

Peter, still groggy from sleep, tries to make up for it all in one moment of courage. He grabs a sword and swings. But Jesus stops him.

"Put up again thy sword into his place," He says. "Thinkest thou that I cannot now pray to my Father...?"

This wasn't a moment for violence. It was the moment for which He had come.

Jesus restrains. Not just Peter. Himself.

He could have called angels. He could have ended the story right there. But He doesn't. He walks toward the cross, with purpose. He fulfills His mission—not because others held Him captive, but because love held Him fast.

This is the grace of Gethsemane—not just that Jesus suffered, but that He suffered *alone*, for the very ones who couldn't stay awake. For Peter, who would deny. For James and John, who would flee. For us, who so often mean well but fall short.

He bore their failure. And ours.

The Hour Still Ticks

Jesus' question in Gethsemane isn't a footnote in history. It's an ongoing whisper to the present.

What about *your* hour?

Can you spare an hour for the Savior who sweat blood for you? Can you linger in prayer—not to perform, but to be present? Can you say yes to the nudge to kneel, to be still, to stay in His Word just a little longer?

We are so eager to do great things for God—write books, build platforms, post devotionals. But Jesus still asks for something far more simple, far more sacred: be with Me.

Not fix. Not impress. Not even succeed.
Just be with Me.

There are moments in life—one-hour moments—when God invites us to watch. To sit. To open our eyes and hearts to the weight He carries. Not to change it. Just to be near.

Watching and Waiting—Together

The early church learned from Gethsemane. Paul told the Thessalonians, "Let us not sleep, as do others; but let us watch and be sober." Peter, perhaps remembering his own failure, wrote, "Be sober, be vigilant; because your adversary the devil…"

They had missed their hour once. They didn't want to miss it again.

And they didn't want others to miss it either.

To watch is to say, "I won't miss this moment. I won't let this pass."
It's what lovers do. It's what soldiers do. It's what friends do. And it's what churches must learn to do—together. Corporate watchfulness is no less vital than personal vigilance. The weary world still waits. And the church is called to stay awake.

And When We've Slept Through the Hour

Maybe you've missed your moment.
Maybe you meant to pray. Meant to trust. Meant to stay close.
And you didn't.

Then hear this: Jesus still went to the cross. Still rose from the grave. Still met Peter on the seaside with breakfast and grace.

Your failure to watch doesn't cancel His love.

But it does cost you the moment. The sacred nearness. The invitation that only comes once.

Better to answer now.
Better to rise.
Better to say, "Yes, Lord—I will sit with You."

Closing the Garden Gate

The garden closed behind them.

Jesus walked forward. The disciples ran. But the memory lingered. The silence of that hour—the prayer unheard, the presence missed—remained.

Some friendships are forged in fire. Others are sealed in silence. The bond between Jesus and those sleepy disciples is a testimony to grace.

To a Savior who asked for one hour… and gave His life instead.

The hour passed. The question remains:

"*What, could ye not watch with me one hour?*"

———————————— • ◆ • ————————————

The Answer asks you...

- Have you grown too weary to watch with Jesus in prayer?
- What "one-hour" moments have you missed because of distraction or fatigue?
- Are you more focused on doing for Christ than simply being with Him?
- How does Jesus' restraint in Gethsemane shape your view of His love and mission?
- In what ways can your church "watch with Him" in a weary and distracted world?

CHAPTER ELEVEN

The Question of Abandonment and Redemption

"And about the ninth hour Jesus cried with a loud voice, saying, Eli, Eli, lama sabachthani? that is to say, My God, my God, why hast thou forsaken me?"
—MATTHEW 27:46

————————— • ◆ • —————————

It was Passover—but the heavens were in mourning.

Jerusalem, usually festive and bursting with ritual, now pulsed with unease. A hush beneath the noise. A shadow beneath the sun. Somewhere outside the city gates, atop a skull-shaped hill called Golgotha, the Lamb of God was preparing to die.

The Trade That Tells the Story

Before Jesus ever reached the cross, a question hovered in the air like incense in the temple courts: whom will you release?

Barabbas or Jesus?

The crowd didn't hesitate. Barabbas was a killer, a rebel, a man of scars and sin. But he was theirs. Jesus was something else—quiet, unsettling, royal without robes. The governor gave the people a choice, and they chose the criminal.

And Jesus said nothing.

Barabbas was guilty—but so were we. And in every heart that's been set free by grace, his name echoes still. The innocent One took the place of the guilty. It wasn't just a swap on a Roman stage. It was a gospel in miniature. Barabbas walks away, bewildered and unshackled, while the Son of God steps into his chains.

This was not the injustice of man—it was the mercy of Heaven.

A Crown That Cut More Than Flesh

They dressed Him like a king.

A scarlet robe, a thorny crown, a reed for a scepter. The soldiers staged their parody with the cruel delight of men too familiar with death. "Hail, King of the Jews!" they sneered, spitting and striking as they bowed with mock reverence.

But what they meant for scorn, Heaven meant for truth.

He was a King. Not of palaces, but of hearts. Not of conquest, but of sacrifice. He wore their shame so we could wear His righteousness. He bore their thorns so we might bear His name. Every wound they inflicted crowned Him with authority they could not fathom.

What they mocked, angels worshipped.

The Silence That Speaks Volumes

From the palace steps to the hill of execution, Jesus spoke little.

When accused, He didn't defend. When mocked, He didn't protest. When stripped, He didn't shrink. Like a lamb led to slaughter, He opened not His mouth. The silence unnerved Pilate. It inflamed the mob. But it resounded through the courts of Heaven like thunder.

Jesus was not powerless. He was purposeful.

Every step, every blow, every breath held restraint. The power that calmed storms, healed fevers, and raised the dead now chose silence. Not because He lacked words. But because love has a language beyond speech.

The silence of Christ was not weakness—it was will. It was the obedience of a Son who would not flinch beneath the weight of our rebellion.

The Weight of the Cross—and the World

They nailed Him to the wood.
And at the sixth hour—high noon—the world turned upside down. The sun dimmed. The shadows deepened. For three hours, darkness swallowed the land, like a veil pulled across creation. Then, at the ninth hour, the silence broke with a cry that still echoes across the centuries:

"My God, my God, why hast thou forsaken me?"

It wasn't whispered. It wasn't mumbled. It was cried. From lungs nearly collapsed and a heart nearly burst. It was the cry of every soul that's ever wondered where God went. The cry of abandonment. Of despair. Of dereliction.

And yet—it was Scripture.

Jesus spoke the first line of Psalm 22. David's ancient lament. A psalm that begins in agony but ends in triumph. But in that moment, Jesus wasn't preaching—He was plunging into the very experience the psalm foretold.

And it's worth noting: this is the only recorded prayer of Jesus where He doesn't address God as "Father." Every other time He prayed—whether in the garden, by the tomb, or in the upper room—He said "Father." But not here. Here, He says, "My God."

Because the cross broke their communion—so ours could be restored.
The Father did not abandon the Son in essence, but for that

moment, Christ entered the full experience of separation that sin deserves.

He bore it for you.
For me.

He who was always with the Father, who shared glory before the foundation of the world, now bore the cold silence of sin's judgment. The Trinity did not fracture—but Jesus willingly endured the felt absence of the Father's face, so you and I would never have to experience it.

The Curtain Tore and the Earth Trembled

And then, He died.

Not collapsed. Not executed. He yielded up the ghost. Gave up His spirit. Surrendered willingly. The Giver of life gave His own.

And the world responded.

The curtain in the temple tore from top to bottom. Not from Earth to Heaven—but from Heaven to Earth. As if God Himself reached down and ripped the veil. The barrier that separated man from God was undone—not by priest or prophet—but by the blood of the Lamb.

The earth shook. Rocks split. Tombs stirred. Death began to unravel, thread by thread.

And a Roman centurion—battle-hardened, blood-splattered—looked up and confessed what the priests would not:

"Truly this was the Son of God."

The Burial That Could Not Hold Him

The body was claimed by Joseph of Arimathea.

He was a man of means and quiet conviction, who had once followed Jesus from the shadows. Now, he stepped into the light. He wrapped the Savior in linen, laid Him in a tomb carved from stone, and rolled the rock into place.

The priests, remembering His promise, pleaded for guards. "Lest His disciples come by night," they said. Pilate gave them what they asked. A seal. A watch. A fortress of stone.

But Heaven was not done.

Though Matthew 27 ends in silence, it leans toward a sunrise where death itself will blink in disbelief. The stone will roll. The grave will gasp. And the One they crucified will walk out—not in weakness, but in resurrection power.

The sky will open wide again.

Jesus Is the Answer

On the cross, Jesus asked the question every heart has asked in the darkness: "Why hast Thou forsaken Me?"

He asked it not because He didn't know the answer—but because we didn't. He asked it to make room for every wounded cry, every whispered doubt, every silent prayer. And He endured the silence of God so we might never be silenced by sin.

He is the Answer.

To loneliness. To guilt. To pain. To death.

The cross does not tidy up suffering. It redeems it. And in the hour when the world turned dark, the Light of the world offered Himself completely—not as victim, but as Victor. Not as a martyr, but as Messiah.

And because He was forsaken, we are forgiven.

———————— • ◆ • ————————

The Answer Asks You...

- Have you ever felt abandoned by God? What did you do with the silence?
- Barabbas walked free because Jesus took his place. Do you live in the awareness that Christ took yours?
- When life feels mocked or misunderstood, do you trust the quiet authority of Christ's kingship?

- The veil was torn to give you access to God. Are you living as if the way is still blocked—or as if it's been opened wide?
- What part of the Cross speaks to your heart most today—and what will you do with it?

CHAPTER TWELVE

The Question of Sorrow and the Hope of Resurrection

Jesus saith unto her, Woman, why weepest thou? whom seekest thou? She, supposing him to be the gardener, saith unto him, Sir, if thou have borne him hence, tell me where thou hast laid him, and I will take him away.

—JOHN 20:15

· ◆ ·

It was still early. The sun had not yet burned the dew from the garden path. Morning light filtered softly through the trees, but the silence was heavy—broken only by the quiet sobs of a woman searching for a body. She had come to grieve. Instead, she would be met with a question that would begin to heal her soul.

When the World Ends in Tears

Mary Magdalene stood outside the tomb, her heart torn open by sorrow. This wasn't just the death of a beloved teacher—it was the unraveling of everything she had come to believe. Jesus had rescued her once—from torment, from shame, from a life in ruins. With a word, He had restored her. With a name, He had claimed her.

But now that voice was silent. The One who had brought her back to life lay buried behind a stone. Or so she thought. And with every passing moment, she feared she would never hear Him speak her name again.

Now, she feared she'd never hear that voice again.

In the fading gray of early morning, she stooped to look into the tomb, expecting only silence and decay. But what she saw startled her—two angels in white, sitting where His body had been. One at the head. One at the feet.

They asked her, almost gently, "Woman, why weepest thou?"

It was a question that sounded like kindness, but it met her in the raw ache of despair. She answered, not with hope, but with loss: "Because they have taken away my Lord, and I know not where they have laid him."

She turned, tears blurring her vision, and there stood a man— silent, steady.

He asked her the same question.

"Woman, why weepest thou?"

The Question that Cuts Through Grief

Jesus did not first reveal Himself. He did not explain the resurrection or roll out angels and trumpets in a spectacle of glory. He asked a question. A tender, piercing question.

Why?

Why are you crying?

This is the question that doesn't scold or accuse. It listens. It leans in. It waits for the heart to answer—not just with words, but with all the weight behind them.

Mary answered, still blind to who stood before her: "Sir, if thou have borne him hence, tell me where thou hast laid him, and I will take him away."

It's a striking moment. She is speaking to the Answer and asking for directions. She is aching for a body and missing the presence of life Himself.

Her sorrow made her eyes slow to see. Her grief distorted reality. And yet, Jesus remained.

He stood in the space between her heartbreak and her healing. And then He said it.

"Mary."

The Sound That Breaks the Silence

Sometimes, all it takes is the sound of your name.

Spoken by the right voice.

She turned fully now—not just physically, but spiritually. Her heart leaped in recognition. Her breath caught. And from her soul erupted one word—"Rabboni!"—a cry of joy and reverence, the old term of affection for her teacher.

The resurrection became personal.

It wasn't just that the tomb was empty. It was that He spoke her name.

And in that moment, grief unraveled. Death reversed. Hope returned.

She had come to anoint a corpse.

She left commissioned to announce a King.

Don't Hold On—Go and Tell

Jesus, ever the gentle Shepherd, calmed her impulse to cling. "Touch me not," He said, "for I am not yet ascended to my Father."

The language here suggests more than physical touch. It implies a clinging—a desire to hold tight and never let go. Who could blame her?

But resurrection doesn't mean things go back to how they were.

Jesus was not returning to His old place beside His disciples. He was ascending to the right hand of the Father. The kingdom was expanding. The mission was widening.

So He gave her a charge: "Go to my brethren, and say unto them, I ascend unto my Father, and your Father; and to my God, and your God."

In essence: Don't stay here, clinging to the old. Step forward. Speak up. The message must go out.

And Mary did.

She became the first witness of the resurrection. The first preacher of Easter. The first to say with trembling voice, "I have seen the Lord."

The Gentle Shepherd Who Knows Your Name

It's tempting to gloss over Mary's tears as simply emotional. But her sorrow represents something deeper.

She is every one of us who has stood beside a grave we didn't expect. Every one of us who has watched a dream dissolve in the early morning fog. Every one of us who has ever wondered where God went when the world fell apart.

And Jesus meets her in that moment. Not with rebuke. Not with spectacle.

With a question.

With presence.

With her name.

He is still that kind of Savior.

He doesn't just raise the dead. He mends the heart.

He is the Answer not only to death, but to despair. Not only to sin, but to sorrow. He is the One who speaks our name when we've forgotten our song.

The One Who Stands Behind You

This story begins the way so many of our stories with Jesus do—not with certainty, but with a quiet awakening. Not with all the answers, but with the unmistakable sense that we are not alone.

Jesus was near, though she didn't see Him at first—just as we often don't. But then He spoke her name, and grace broke through the sorrow.

Isn't that the way grace works?

He doesn't force Himself into our grief. He walks quietly into our garden of despair, waits for us to speak our sorrow, and then speaks to us—not in grand theological terms—but with one word:

Mary.

The question "Why weepest thou?" is not a rebuke for crying. It's an invitation to lift your eyes.

Because behind you stands the risen Christ.

And everything changes when He calls your name.

— • ♦ • —

The Answer asks you...

- What sorrow are you holding that has made it hard to see Jesus standing near?
- If Jesus asked you today, "Why are you weeping?"— how would you answer?
- Have you mistaken Jesus for someone else—someone distant, absent, or uninterested?
- Are you clinging to what was, instead of stepping into what Jesus is calling you to now?
- When was the last time you recognized Jesus calling your name in the middle of your pain?

CHAPTER THIRTEEN

The Question of Love That Restores and Sends

> "So when they had dined, Jesus saith to Simon Peter, Simon, son of Jonas, lovest thou me more than these? He saith unto him, Yea, Lord; thou knowest that I love thee. He saith unto him, Feed my lambs."
>
> —JOHN 21:15

———— • ◆ • ————

The morning mist hovered low over the waters of Galilee, soft and gray like a blanket pulled gently over the shoreline. The waves whispered against the rocks with a rhythm only the weary could hear. A fire crackled nearby, its smoke rising in thin threads toward the pale dawn. Around it, seven men sat quietly, not yet fully speaking—until He spoke.

Jesus had prepared the meal.

Bread. Fish. And something more.

Peter sat among them, warmed by the fire but chilled by memory. The last time he had been near a fire, it hadn't been for breakfast. It had been for betrayal.

By the Fire Again

The fire crackled in the morning air, smoke curling into the pale light. It warmed the bones but stirred the memory. "I know not the man," Peter had said that night, and he had meant it—until the rooster crowed and regret shattered his resolve. That moment haunted him still.

Now he sat on Galilee's shore, no sword in hand, no promises on his lips—just silence. He wasn't the same man who once stepped out on water or dared to rebuke the Lord. He was quieter. Humbled. Unsure.

Then Jesus turned to him.

"Simon, son of Jonas, lovest thou me more than these?"

Not "Peter." Not "Rock." Just "Simon." His old name. It felt like Jesus was peeling back the layers, going back to the beginning—back to where it all started.

Peter's eyes drifted to the nets, the boats, the friends beside him. Did he love Jesus more than fishing? More than fellowship? More than his failure?

Jesus used a deeper word for love—*agape*. Peter responded with the love he could honestly offer—*phileo*. Not perfect, but real.

"Yea, Lord; thou knowest that I love thee."

Jesus nodded. "Feed my lambs."

The Threefold Question of Love

Jesus asked again: "Simon, son of Jonas, lovest thou me?" This second time, the question cut deeper. Peter remembered the moment he left the nets the first time, full of purpose. But had he ever truly left himself behind?

"Yea, Lord; thou knowest that I love thee."

"Feed my sheep."

Then came the third time—and with it, a subtle shift. Jesus used Peter's word: *phileo*. A gentler word. Not divine *agape*, but brotherly love. It was as if Jesus met Peter right where he was, stooping to the level his heart could reach.

"Simon, son of Jonas, lovest thou me?"

Peter was grieved. Not because the question changed—but because it hadn't. This wasn't accusation. It was restoration. Jesus was doing soul-surgery, touching the tender place where shame still lingered.

"Lord, thou knowest all things; thou knowest that I love thee." Jesus smiled. "Feed my sheep."

Three denials. Three questions. Three commissions. Grace didn't just erase the past—it rewrote it.

A Quiet Call to Follow

Peter didn't yet know what this moment would become. He didn't know that soon he would preach boldly at Pentecost, or pen letters that would comfort a suffering church. He didn't know that tradition would remember him not for his denial, but for dying upside down—unworthy, he said, to be crucified like his Lord.

But Jesus didn't hand him a future. He gave him a calling.

Follow Me.

Not "Fix it all." Not "Prove yourself." Just: **Follow Me.**

Grace That Does More Than Cleanse

All of us have sat where Peter sat. We've made vows on mountaintops and broken them in valleys. We've walked with Jesus in the light, then stumbled in the dark. And we've wondered, like Peter, if the story is over.

But Jesus still builds fires on the shoreline of our shame.

He still invites us to come and eat.

He still asks, "Do you love Me?"

Not "Did you fail?" Not "Are you worthy?" But "Do you love Me?" He wants your heart. Even if it's bruised. Even if it's hesitant. Even if all you can say is, "You know I do."

Because love is the beginning of healing. And healing is the beginning of calling.

"Feed my sheep."

The Question That Heals

Jesus' question wasn't just a test—it was a turning point. "Lovest thou me?" is the question that reaches past behavior and presses into the heart. When love is real—faith follows. Obedience follows. Endurance follows.

Peter didn't pretend to have perfect love. He didn't bluster this time. He simply offered what he had: "You know I love you." And that was enough.

Jesus took that honest affection and planted it in grace. From it would grow a faith bold enough to stand before rulers and gentle enough to shepherd the scattered. A love that once crumbled in fear would become the foundation of courage.

The Fire Is Still Burning

We fail. We fall. We forget. But grace still calls. The same Savior who met Peter by the fire meets us too—with warmth, with bread, with mercy that restores and recommissions.

There is a fire on the shore. There is bread and fish—and forgiveness. There is a question whispered over the waves:

"Do you love Me?"

If you hear that voice today, don't hide. Don't perform. Don't pretend.

Just say, "Lord, you know."

He does.

And He still calls.

Follow me.

—————————— • ◆ • ——————————

The Answer asks you...

- What failure do you still carry that Jesus is ready to redeem?
- How has shame silenced your love for Christ—and how might He be restoring it?
- When Jesus asks, "Do you love Me?" what would an honest answer look like for you?
- Where is Jesus calling you to serve—not to earn grace, but because you've received it?
- Have you accepted His restoration as enough to walk forward again?

CHAPTER FOURTEEN

The Question of Conviction and Transformation

"And he fell to the earth, and heard a voice saying unto him, Saul, Saul, why persecutest thou me?"

—Acts 9:4

• ◆ •

The dust hadn't even settled. Stephen's body still lay broken on the outskirts of Jerusalem, but the story was already shifting. While the faithful mourned a martyr, another man was on the move. Saul of Tarsus, fire in his lungs and fury in his heart, left the scene of the stoning not in sorrow, but with fresh resolve. The man who held the cloaks that day now carried a crusade. He had watched Stephen die. Heard his prayer. Seen his peace. But instead of softening, Saul stiffened. The gospel that comforted the dying enraged the living.

And yet, even as Saul breathed threats, heaven was preparing a question. One that would not only change his direction but reshape history.

The Prayer That Fell Like Seed

The first stones fell like thunder. Stephen, calm and radiant, didn't curse or cry out. He looked up. "I see the heavens opened," he said, "and the Son of Man standing at the right hand of God." That was all it took. The crowd rushed him. They dragged him outside the city and crushed him with rocks.

But Stephen's final breath carried a prayer. "Lord, lay not this sin to their charge." It wasn't just a cry of mercy. It was a seed. And though Saul stood unmoved at the time, heaven heard the prayer. Grace, like rain, waits for the right season.

Scattered, but Not Silenced

Persecution came like a flood. The church scattered, but it didn't scatter in fear. It scattered in mission. The gospel spread from house to house, village to village. Philip preached in Samaria. Believers found refuge in Damascus. But Saul wasn't finished.

He secured warrants, raided homes, tore families apart. He hunted followers of the Way with the zeal of a man convinced he was doing God a favor. But conviction has a way of finding us—even when we're running full speed in the wrong direction.

When Grace Interrupts a Mission

The road to Damascus was dusty, long, and loud with certainty. But at high noon, heaven interrupted.

A light flashed. A presence surrounded. Saul fell.

And then a voice.

"Saul, Saul, why persecutest thou me?"

Not "them." Not "my followers." Me.

The question pierced deeper than the light. It wasn't angry. It wasn't distant. It was personal. Jesus so identifies with His Church that to wound them is to wound Him.

"Who art thou, Lord?" Saul asked.

The answer came: "I am Jesus, whom thou persecutest."

In an instant, Saul saw what he had refused to see. The name he hated was now the voice he couldn't unhear. And with that voice came a truth Saul could no longer kick against.

When Blindness Brings Clarity

The proud Pharisee was now blind. Led by hand into the city, Saul sat in silence for three days. He didn't eat. He didn't drink. He just waited.

And while he waited, another man heard from God.

Ananias was a disciple. Faithful, cautious, and afraid. When the Lord told him to go to Saul, he hesitated. Everyone knew Saul. He was the nightmare made real.

But God said, "He is a chosen vessel unto me."

So Ananias obeyed. He found Saul, placed his hands on him, and said two words that must have melted every wall:

"Brother Saul."

The persecutor was now family.

Scales fell. Sight returned. And the man who came to arrest Christians rose to proclaim Christ.

The Voice That Becomes Your Mission

Saul never got over Damascus. He never got over grace.

He never forgot the question that turned his life around.

"Why persecutest thou me?"

It wasn't condemnation. It was invitation.

From that day forward, Paul would preach the Christ he once opposed. He would write letters from prison cells, plant churches in hostile cities, and suffer gladly for the name he once tried to erase.

He would call himself the chief of sinners—and the recipient of mercy.

The Gospel That Still Turns Lives Around

Acts 9 ends not with Saul's arresting power, but with his escape—lowered in a basket through a city wall, fleeing the very people he once led.

But more than a man changed that day. A movement deepened. A message spread.

And a question still echoes:

"Why are you fighting me?"

Sometimes we don't recognize our resistance as persecution. But we resist all the same.

We push back against conviction. We defend our pride. We run from surrender.

But the Savior who stood in Saul's path still stands in ours. Not to destroy. But to redeem.

The One Who Meets Us on the Road

Jesus meets us not at the destination, but in the dust. On the road. In the middle of our certainty, in the middle of our rebellion.

He asks questions that stop us short and open us up.

Not to shame us. But to save us.

The grace that found Saul wasn't neat or expected. It was disruptive. Blinding. Beautiful.

And it still finds us.

You may think you're too far gone, too resistant, too hard. But Saul would tell you otherwise.

You may think you've got God figured out, boxed in by doctrine or dismissed by doubt. But one question from Jesus can upend a life and reroute a soul.

And so He asks again:

Why are you resisting? Why are you running? Why are you persecuting me?

The voice isn't angry. It's aching.

And it's calling you home.

The Invitation That Changes Everything

The story of Saul is not just a record of history. It is a mirror. A reminder that no one is beyond the reach of grace. That no heart is too hard, no past too stained, no resistance too strong.

Jesus is still meeting people on dusty roads. Still calling them by name. Still asking the question that turns us around.

And if you've heard Him—if somewhere deep inside, you feel the gentle tug of conviction, the stirring of something more— then today is your Damascus road.

Salvation isn't earned. It's received. Saul didn't work his way to God. God came to him. And He's coming to you.

The Bible says, "For all have sinned, and come short of the glory of God" (Romans 3:23). That includes Saul. That includes me. That includes you.

But it also says, "While we were yet sinners, Christ died for us" (Romans 5:8). The very One we've resisted is the One who laid down His life for us.

And it gives us this promise: "That if thou shalt confess with thy mouth the Lord Jesus, and shalt believe in thine heart that God hath raised him from the dead, thou shalt be saved" (Romans 10:9).

Jesus is not waiting for perfection. He's waiting for surrender.

QUESTIONS FROM THE ANSWER

Will you trust Him today? Will you say, like Saul once did, "Lord, what wilt thou have me to do?"

There's no magic formula. Just an honest heart. A whispered prayer. Something like this:

Lord Jesus, I know I'm a sinner. I know I've resisted You. But I believe You died for me, and I believe You rose again. I trust You now as my Savior and Lord. Forgive me. Change me. Lead me. I am Yours.

If you prayed those words and meant them, you've begun the greatest journey of your life. Like Saul, you've gone from blindness to sight. From running to resting. From death to life.

And you've met the Answer—not just to your questions, but to your soul.

Welcome home.

———————— • ◆ • ————————

The Answer asks you...

- Are there ways you're resisting the pricks of conviction in your own life?
- Do you see the Church as deeply connected to Christ—or as just another institution?
- How does Jesus' question to Saul reshape your view of divine mercy and personal repentance?
- Who in your life seems beyond the reach of grace—and how does Saul's story challenge that belief?
- Have you ever allowed a painful confrontation with truth to become a turning point of grace?

CHAPTER FIFTEEN

The Voice That Never Fades

The tomb is still empty. The stone is still removed. The scars still testify. And though centuries have passed since Jesus walked dusty roads and calmed stormy seas, His voice still lingers—strong enough to steady the trembling, soft enough to stir the soul. His questions still echo across generations. But hear this: the Answer still speaks.

Not with the thunder of Sinai or the fury of the whirlwind, but in the quiet places where hearts ache and questions hang in the air like morning mist. He speaks when the room is empty and the diagnosis is full. When the marriage is breaking and the bank account is broken. When hope falters and faith flickers. His voice—like a river in drought season—finds the cracks. Finds you.

He speaks—first and always—through His Word. Every line of Scripture is His breath on the page, inspired and unchanging. But His voice does not fall silent when the Bible is closed. He guides by His truth through faithful preaching, and sometimes He echoes it in unexpected places: a whisper in a hospital hallway, a shaft of sunlight across a kitchen floor, a lyric that arrives at just the right moment. He speaks to the doubter, the dreamer, the deconstructed, and the disillusioned. And when He speaks, it isn't to shame or scold—it's to call. To remind. To love.

Because the Answer is not just a doctrine. Not a moral code or a creedal line. The Answer is a Person. And that Person is alive. He speaks to the Martha who wonders if serving is enough. To the Peter who sank in the sea of his own ambition. To the Thomas who needs more than secondhand faith. To the Mary who weeps because hope seems buried. But when the Answer speaks, graves lose their grip. Doubt bows to truth. Hearts burn with recognition.

The questions He asked then—He asks still. "What seek ye?" still speaks to the one searching in all the wrong places. "Lovest thou me?" still whispers into the shame of the one who failed Him. "Why are ye fearful?" still meets the midnight panic of the one lying awake, wondering how it will all work out. His questions disarm us. Not because He doesn't know the answer—but because He knows we don't, and He wants to walk with us while we find it.

His questions are invitations. Behind each one stands a Savior with open arms. Not just for the holy, but for the hurting. Not just for the faithful, but for the fallen.

Maybe that's what the world needs most now. Not louder arguments. Not shinier slogans. Not more content to scroll past. But a quiet return to the voice of Jesus. A listening for the Word made flesh, the Lamb who was slain, the Shepherd who knows His sheep. Maybe you and I are called to go on as echoes of His voice in a world that's forgotten what grace sounds like.

Go on listening. Go on trusting. Go on becoming the kind of person through whom the Answer still speaks.

He still speaks in the stillness of dawn and the weariness of night. When your plans collapse. When prayers go unanswered. When you feel forgotten or found out. When the funeral is fresh and the silence feels permanent. Even then, especially then—He speaks. And when He speaks, it is enough.

Because He is still Emmanuel. God with us.

And His voice is not always loud, but it is always near.

So let this final word not be goodbye, but a beginning. Go on listening. Go on loving. Go on becoming an echo of His voice in a world still aching for grace. And remember—His voice is never far.

It may come through Scripture in the morning or a song in the evening. Through the smile of a stranger or the silence of surrender. But when He speaks, you'll know it. Your spirit will rise. Your soul will settle. And something deep inside you will remember: this is what truth sounds like. This is what love sounds like. This is what hope sounds like.

And if you still your soul, and still your mind, you will hear Him again—because the Answer still speaks.

And He's speaking now.

Thank you for listening to the questions from the Answer with me. This journey has been more than ink on a page—it's been a quiet walk toward the voice of Jesus. I haven't written from a place of having all the answers, but from a deep longing to follow the One who is the Answer. If these questions have drawn you closer to His voice, then we've walked this road well together. May we never stop listening for Him—because He has never stopped speaking.

www.ingramcontent.com/pod-product-compliance
Lightning Source LLC
Chambersburg PA
CBHW030515100426
42813CB00001B/49